Little Bo-Peep

to the Sloan Flock

Ticknor & Fields, a Houghton Mifflin Company
Copyright © 1986 by Paul Galdone
All rights reserved. Printed in Italy

Library of Congress Cataloging in Publication Data
Galdone, Paul.
Little-Bo-peep.
Summary: An illustrated rendition of the traditional
nursery rhyme about the little girl who lost her sheep.
1. Nursery rhymes.   2. Children's poetry.
[1. Nursery rhymes]   I. Title.
PZ8.3.G1218Li   1986   398'.8   85-14914
ISBN 0-89919-395-1

NI 10 9 8 7 6 5 4 3 2 1

Little Bo-Peep

Illustrated by

PAUL GALDONE

CLARION BOOKS

TICKNOR & FIELDS : A HOUGHTON MIFFLIN COMPANY
NEW YORK

1739

Little Bo-peep has lost her sheep,
And doesn't know where to find them.

Leave them alone,
And they'll come home,
Bringing their tails behind them.

Little Bo-peep fell fast asleep,

And dreamt
She heard them bleating.

But when she awoke,
She found it a joke,
For they were still a-fleeting.

Then up she took her little crook,
Determined for to find them.

She found them indeed,
But it made her heart bleed,

For they'd left their tails
Behind them.

Now it happened one day,
As Bo-peep did stray
Into a meadow close by,

That there she espied
Their tails side by side,
All hung on a tree to dry.

She heaved a sigh,
And wiped her eye,
And over the hillocks
Went rambling,

And tried what she could,
As a shepherdess should,